COLLECTORS' PIECES 7

DELFTWARE

John Bedford

WALKER AND COMPANY
NEW YORK

Library of Congress Catalog Card Number: 66–22378

First published in the United States of America in 1966 by Walker and Company, a division of Publications Development Corporation

Printed in Great Britain

Contents

Introduction

Once upon a time I was a fairly frequent caller at a certain antique 'shop' which stood upon one of the levels of that romantic staircase in Bristol called Christmas Steps. I put the word 'shop' in quotes because the inscription on the faded facia board read 'Antique *Collector*'.

The place resembled a second-hand furniture store, but when you looked inside his cupboards and chests of drawers, you saw what 'Old Elson', as the owner liked to be called, meant by the word '*Collector*'. He would as soon talk about these treasures as sell you any; and if he let you have a piece he would be careful to keep tabs on you so that one day he could buy it back.

'Old Elson' has long since passed on, but there must be several generations of collectors into whose hands he was the first to place a piece of English delftware. For the admirer of Chelsea or Dresden, or even his beloved Champion's Bristol porcelain, it was a big jump. Here was a coarse earthenware, bearing bold, sometimes crude, decoration in vigorous colours. It belonged not to the Chippendale china cabinet but to the open court cupboard and the 'delft rack'. English delftware is an acquired taste, but when it makes converts it usually keeps them.

Delftware also offers a more sophisticated satisfaction in the Dutchman's version. His word 'porseleyn' invited comparison with Chinese porcelain and it was no idle boast.

This little book tries to give a sketch in words and pictures of both kinds, showing their similarities and their differences; and also relating them to their times and to the great family of tin-glazed earthenware.

ENGLISH DELFTWARE

1. What is Delftware?

Let us begin with a few definitions. 'Delftware' is the name given in England and other English-speaking countries to a kind of pottery which is neither porcelain (like Sèvres or Dresden), nor china (like old Spode), nor stoneware (like a Bellarmine jug).

It is a fairly soft earthenware covered with a glaze of lead made opaque with ashes or oxide of tin. On this white absorbent surface the decorator paints his pattern or picture swiftly and irrevocably, as though he were working in watercolour. The technique calls for a sure instinct and in this form it gives a result totally different from the 'tight' work of the porcelain painter. In the Netherlands, as we shall see, there were refinements on the process: the design might be covered with a second lead glaze to give richness and depth and the whole fired together at a high temperature. Other and more sensitive colours might then be added and the piece fired again at a lower temperature in a 'muffle' kiln. The process is called enamelling, and is comparable with similar work on the china, porcelain and opaque glass which this kind of delftware was designed to emulate.

The family of tin-glazed earthenware is a large one; its history begins, not, as is often thought, with the Netherlands town of Delft, but in Moorish Spain and Renaissance Italy. Through Majorca—so acquiring the name maiolica, or majolica—there came into Italy shipments of magnificent wares with lustred and other decoration which caught the imagination of Italian potters at such centres as Orvieto and Faenza. This inspired them to make similar wares in their own styles, classical in conception, but with more than a touch of exotic ideas from the Near and Middle East and Ming dynasty China.

Customers at a delftware shop, mid-eighteenth century. (H. Harvard's *La Céramique Hollandaise.*)

From Italy the art of maiolica spread through Europe, its rise being greatly stimulated by competition with the ever-increasing flow of porcelains from the Far East. In Germany, France and other northern countries it became known as *faience* or *fayence*, after the town of Faenza, one of the first centres to send shipments of the wares round to northern waters, probably on the regular galley services run by the Venetians. This method of transport may have contributed another name to tin-glazed earthenware. In the Netherlands its makers—as distinct from other kinds of potters—became known as *geleyerspotbakkers*; and the expressions galleypot-makers and galleywares crossed the North Sea to acquire usage in England. Not twenty miles from where I write, in Sussex, there is a country lane called Gallipot Street which has recently yielded to the busy fingers of local children evidence of having been the site of an old pottery.

What we now call 'delftware' was made in England and Flanders long before the rise of Delft as a pottery centre. For the beginnings of tin-glazed earthenware in Europe one looks in fact to Antwerp rather than the Dutch centres. A maiolica maker called Guido Andries who flourished there about 1512 is believed to be the same Guido da Savino who worked at Castel Durante; and not only did his family spread to the northern Netherlands towns, but his son or grandson came to London and started a pottery there.

At first both the English and the Netherlandish wares, whether made by immigrants or natives, were heavily influenced in their styles by the Italian imports; and for this class of wares the collector today uses, respectively, the terms English maiolica or *Nederlandse majolica.* Later, both countries gradually adopted new styles based either on Chinese porcelain as seen in the K'ang Hsi period or on themes native to each country, e.g. landscapes, flower painting or genre pictures. For these, the Dutch themselves seem now to favour the terms *Delfts aardewerk* or *fayence*, but I have elected to follow the erudite Sotheby cataloguer in using the English expression 'Dutch delft'. On the same authority I call our own version 'English delftware'.

It may be useful at this point to deal with some terms which many tyro collectors have found misleading. In nineteenth-century England, potters like Mintons, Wedgwood, Doultons, and Copeland made large quantities of earthenware and stoneware decorated with coloured glazes in the styles of the Palissy wares of the sixteenth century and of Chinese self-coloured wares. These, by some strange quirk, they decided to name 'majolica' or 'faience'. A

English maiolica jug, perhaps made at Southwark, 1632. (Victoria and Albert Museum.)

Lambeth vase, decorated in polychrome, c. *1700.* (Sotheby and Co.)

great deal of it is to be found on oldfashioned town halls and public lavatories; and anything less like maiolica or faience it is difficult to imagine.

The word 'delftware' itself is often used on modern imitations, usually seen as gift china—for example, small Dutch figures in 'national' costume. These pieces are in a hard-fired earthenware covered with a slip and painted under a lead glaze. It is nothing like the work done on the porous tin glaze and the inscription 'delftware' is in fact a guarantee that it is nothing of the kind.

On the other hand, there are careful imitations of early delftware which present real problems to the collector, and some remarks on these are offered on page 64.

Marks on delftware are many, but often misleading. The Dutch potters used initials and sometimes symbols to distinguish their wares, but some of the earlier attributions have since been shown to be unreliable. The most up-to-date authorities in English are W. B. Honey and J. B. Cushion (*Handbook of Pottery and Porcelain Marks*). Very little in the way of marking was done on English delftware, but the exceptions are dealt with in the appropriate place.

LEFT

(Above, left to right)

Flowerholder and plaque printed in blue and manganese purple. Delft, eighteenth century.

Little girl in a high chair, painted in colours, Mark 'Jv Duijn' for Johannes van Duijn at the 'Porcelain Dish' factory, c. *1765.*

(Below, left to right)

Teapot painted in colours on black enamel, Mark 'LVE' in monogram and '5' in yellow. Early eighteenth century.

Dish painted in high-temperature colours with chinoiserie *and on the rim two views of Dutch villages in blue reserved on a ground of floral ornament. 15¼ in. diameter. Mid-eighteenth century.*

Inkstand in the form of a boat, rowed by a man and steered by a woman, with the inkpot in the form of a butter-tub, painted in colours. Mid-eighteenth century. (All from the Fitzwilliam Museum, Cambridge)

RIGHT
(Above, left to right)
Plate painted in colours with chinoiserie. *Lambeth,* c. *1760.*

Blue-dash Tulip Charger painted in colours. Lambeth, late seventeenth century.

Plate painted in colours in the centre and with bianco sopra bianco *decoration round the rim. Bristol, eighteenth century.*

(Below, left to right)
Wall bracket in the form of a cornucopia, moulded in relief and painted in 'Fazackerly' colours; dish with the same decoration, 18 in. diameter. Both Liverpool, c. *1760.*

Mug painted in white on a bleu de Nevers *enamel background. Lambeth, late seventeenth century.*
(All from the Fitzwilliam Museum, Cambridge)

2. The Potters

(*a*) LAMBETH

The first galleypot-makers known by name in England are two men from Antwerp, Jacob Janson and Jasper Andries, the latter said to have been the son or grandson of the Guido Andries who migrated from Castel Durante to Antwerp. These partners first settled in Norwich in 1567; but later, complaining that they were having great trouble in finding materials suitable for making their 'galley paving tiles and vessels for apothecaries and others', they petitioned Queen Elizabeth for permission to move to London.

By 1571 they had established themselves at Aldgate, at the eastern end of the city, and as time went on more potters, both English and Flemish or Dutch, settled in the same district. There was another pottery called the Hermitage near St Katherine's Dock; and south of the river, at Pickleherring Quay in the parish of St Olaves', Southwark, there was a pottery owned by one Christian Wilhelm. He was working about 1625, and described himself as galleypot maker to Charles I. Wilhelm is said to have been concerned in the making of smalt, the cobalt blue pigment used for painting on the wares, and he had connections with a pottery near Southwark Cathedral. There was also a pottery of some sort at Vauxhall.

No tin-glazed earthenware seems to have been made at Lambeth itself until about 1665, when a Dutchman from Delft, John Ariens van Hamme, established himself there and took out a patent for making 'tiles and porcelain after the way practised in Holland'. 'Porcelain' here stands for *porseleyn*, in the sense already mentioned in the Introduction.

Lambeth harvest jug, with Chinese and English motifs, 1699. (Sotheby and Co.)

From this time—in other words the 'delftware' era as distinct from that of maiolica—Lambeth took the lead among the London galleyware-makers; and its name stands for the wares made at all these centres, now practically impossible to distinguish from each other.

The Lambeth sites are rich in shards or wasters, and this has helped to identify much locally made ware. The late Professor Garner also established that the body of the earliest Lambeth wares, from before 1680–90, was usually white, although some had a pinkish tone, due perhaps to the potters having fired them near some coloured wares. The later Lambeth, however, has a greenish-blue tint. More will be noted about the differences in types and styles of the various centres as we discuss the wares themselves.

(*b*) BRISTOL AND WINCANTON

Bristol has been a centre for all kinds of pottery and glass for centuries, and it offers us more names of actual galley-ware-makers and painters than any other. But the job of attaching the names to particular wares remains tantalizingly difficult: today we are far less confident of identifying the work of such men as Joseph Flower, John Niglett or John Bowen than were the ceramic historians of the nineteenth century, who were apt to make guesses on very little evidence. On the other hand a great deal of invaluable research has been done by the late Professor Garner, Mr van Oss and others, which has taught us much about the styles and types of wares made at Bristol.

The West Country seems to have found its first galleyware-makers about the year 1650. They worked not in the city of Bristol itself but in the neighbouring village of Brislington—now a suburb. A pottery appears to have been founded there by two men from Southwark, John Bissicke and Robert Fleming, perhaps from the Low Countries. It was built into the ancient site of a medieval chapel dedicated to St Anne, near the River Avon.

Just before the First World War excavations were carried

(Left) *Delftware plate claimed as the work of Michael Edkins of Bristol, with* (below) *date and initials, perhaps for Edkins and his wife 'Betty'* (see p. 19). (Hugh Owen's *Two Centuries of Ceramic Art in Bristol.*) (Centre) *Delftware plate said to have been painted by Joseph Flower of Bristol, with* (below) *date and initials, perhaps for Flower and his wife Sarah* (see p. 15). (L. Jewett's *Ceramic Art in Great Britain.*) (Right) *Delftware plate, with* (below) *John Bowen's signature: a key piece for his style. 14 in. in diameter* (see p. 18). (*Ceramic Art in Great Britain.*)

out at Brislington by Mr W. J. Pountney, and an account of his findings was published in his *Old Bristol Potteries*. He found a great many fragments of polychrome and blue and white delftwares, some of them bearing dates like 1652 and 1653. They were perhaps made by that 'Robert Collins, of Brislington, potter' whose name appears in a deed of property concerning a field on the site. Other Brislington potters whose names appear on records are Matthew Wilcox, Edward Mearn (of a very long-lived family of Bristol potters) and Edward Ward. The latter, a freeman of the city of Bristol, continued as proprietor at Brislington until 1697, when he relinquished that concern to his pupil, Thomas Frank, and set up kilns in Bristol itself. Nine years later Frank followed his erstwhile master there, taking premises at Redcliff Backs, and was succeeded at Brislington by Thomas Dixon. By about 1735–50 this pottery was being carried on by Thomas Taylor, a Dixon apprentice, in partnership with a brother named Hugh and a Richard Riley. Eventually they too, departed for Bristol and by the 1770s the pottery had become a bakery.

E
M·B
1760

ye 1st Septr
1761
Bowen fecit

(Left) *Plate painted in the 'John Bowen' style. Bristol,* c. *1760.* (Victoria and Albert Museum.)
(Right) *Plate made for a Dutch ship, with* bianco sopra bianco *decoration. Bristol,* c. *1760.* (Victoria and Albert Museum.)

Further excavations made at Brislington during the 'thirties by Mr H. W. Maxwell brought to light another cache of wasters. These revealed that Brislington produced its quota of the well-known circular salt-cellars, sometimes with ball-feet, porringers or bleeding bowls having the single five-lobed half-star handles with a central hole, small drug jars and cylindrical mugs.

Edward Ward had been making galleywares at Bristol some years before he left Brislington, working at Temple Backs in partnership with his three sons. He died in 1709 a wealthy man, and in his will there is mention of a house at Westbury-on-Trym where there is—or was in Pountney's day—a dairy or larder lined with tiles painted in the style usually attributed to John Bowen (pp. 11 and 12), who worked at the Temple Pottery. Not many opportunities have occurred for excavations on the Temple Backs site, but from time to time pieces of tiles have been found with manganese purple grounds and decoration in reserved panels. The Temple pottery passed through several hands and the concern still survives at Fishponds as the Bristol Pottery.

The Redcliff Backs pottery, established by Thomas Frank of Brislington in 1706, was carried on by his son Richard until 1777, when he transferred to Temple Backs, working there until his death in 1785. Much important delftware has been attributed to this pottery, but only on the slenderest evidence.

A further centre for galleyware potting in Bristol was on the other side of the Avon, past College Green and on the beginning of the old footpath to Clifton. Here was the Limekiln Lane pottery—or rather two potteries which were usually in the hands of the same owners. They were founded somewhere between 1700 and 1706, and the record of apprenticeship there of the aptly named William Pottery reveals that in 1706 Limekiln Lane was owned by a partnership consisting of Henry Hobbs, a practical potter, and Woodes Rogers, the famous sea-captain and privateer commander, who rescued from the island of Juan Fernandez the marooned mariner Alexander Selkirk, original of Defoe's Robinson Crusoe. Crusoe himself, it will be recalled, tried his hand at potting, producing, as he says, 'three very good, I will not say handsome, pipkins: and two other earthenware pots, as hard burn't as could be desired; and one of them perfectly glazed with the running of the sand'. Defoe, it may not be generally known, was for a time manager of a pantile factory near Tilbury.

Hobbs was succeeded at Limekiln Lane about 1724 by a John Weaver, upon whose death in 1735 William Pottery fulfilled the promise of his name by taking over the business until his death in 1742, when he was followed by an apprentice of his, Joseph Bundy. A few years later potting ceased at Limekiln Lane and the premises were sold.

Some excavations carried out between the wars by Mr Maxwell at a near-by quarry, which was also used by the potters for tipping rubbish, yielded fragments which showed that as well as the cobalt blue, the potters used a pale yellow, a red and a pale dull green. Tiles and bowls made there were painted in purple but always in combination with blue. On the bowls this colouring was faint, but on some of the plates it was brilliant, especially the reds and greens. The largest

plates bore numbers on the backs, one specimen having two.

Features of these Limekiln Lane wasters are seen on shards found at Wincanton, Somerset, and in fact this establishment may almost be regarded as another Bristol Factory. Thomas Lindslee, an apprentice of Pottery's at Limekiln Lane, was associated with it, also Nathaniel Ireson (1686–1769), whose name, together with the date 1748, appears on a fragment found by Pountney on the Wincanton site. Pountney offers no evidence that Ireson was a potter, and in fact the inscription on his tomb describes him as a builder. There is a jug in the Fitzwilliam Museum with decoration similar to that of the Wincanton shard.

Candlesticks were a special feature of the work at Wincanton. There are also in existence four plates bearing the place name and the years 1737, 1738, and 1739; but although competently painted they show no evidence of any marked factory style.

Before leaving the West Country factories, more must be said about that Joseph Flower who was apprenticed to Thomas Frank at Redcliff Backs in 1763. A great deal of work has been attributed to him, but although he is described as a potter on the occasion of his second marriage and again when he died, nobody has ever really established that he was a master potter in his own right: there is no record, for example, of his ever having taken an apprentice.

Flower had a shop or warehouse at No. 2

Bristol tiles, showing various styles of decoration, eighteenth century. (Victoria and Albert Museum.)

The Quay, which was next to 'Small Street Gate' on the banks of what was then the River Frome. This is attested by a notice in *Felix Farley's Journal* for 26 April, 1767.

At the time of his death in 1785, Flower was living in Corn Street and had his warehouse there, as is shown by an advertisement in the *Bristol Gazatte* for 23 February, 1786.

It now seems reasonable to assume, therefore, that although he started life as a potter, Joseph Flower was for most of his life a wholesale and retail merchant in pottery, porcelain and glass, selling not only the wares of Bristol but also those of Liverpool and Staffordshire. He may well have commissioned work from the local potteries—for example the bowls made for foreign ships entering the port (p. 35)—which would explain the reference to him in the records as a potter.

What, then, are we to make of the pieces, some of them bearing Flower's name or initials, which have been handed down in his family as the handiwork of himself or his employees at the shadowy factory at Redcliff Backs?

First, there is the bowl signed 'Joseph Flower, sculpt., 1747'. It is in blue monochrome, $12\frac{3}{4}$ in. in diameter across the top and $8\frac{3}{4}$ in. high. There are four panels, showing a pastoral scene, a group of men drinking and smoking, a seascape with a naval action, etc. Its most interesting feature, however, is that inside the bowl are the words and music for a 'rota' or song by Purcell. Pountney traced it to an

(Left) *Plate painted in manganese purple. Wincanton, 1740.* (Victoria and Albert Museum.)
(Right) *Plate painted in powder purple and blue, showing Justice trampling on Tyranny, with the motto 'Libertas Populi', commemorating Wilkes and the* North Briton. *Wincanton,* c. *1760.* (Sotheby and Co.)

old book published by R. Broderick in 1795, *A Collection of Duets, Rotas, Canons, Catches and Glees, selected for and most respectfully inscribed to the Members of the Bristol Catch Club and the Cecilian Society.* At the date on this bowl, Flower would have been about twenty-four years of age, and well out of his apprenticeship: but unless he worked for a spell as an engraver, it is difficult to account for the 'sculpt'.

Then there are two large chargers painted in blue with a view of the bombardment of Chagre, on the coast of Panama. These commemorate the famous action fought by Admiral Vernon in recapturing Portobello from the Spaniards: the event will be well known to collectors of Staffordshire wares. The two chargers were sold by Flower's descendants to Dr William Glaisher: one of them is in the magnificent collection of tin-glazed earthenware which he bequeathed to the Fitzwilliam Museum at Cambridge; the other is in the Victoria and Albert Museum. It bears the date 1740, which is perhaps that of an engraving from which the picture was taken, for the engagement took place in 1739.

Another documentary piece attributed to Flower, also in

the Fitzwilliam, and again no very great shakes artistically, is a plate bearing a copy of the title-page of a book called *The Man in the Moone* by Domingo Gonsales, a pseudonym for Francis Godwin, Bishop of Hereford. This bears the initials and date 'I.F. 1740'; and the same initials appear on pieces with other dates.

Another mark suggested as being connected with Flower shows the triangular marriage initials J S F 1750, (p. 11), alleged to be those of Joseph Flower and his wife Sarah; but according to the registers of St Mary Redcliff the couple had their first son eight years before this date. It will be unnecessary to point out to those familiar with porcelain and pottery from other centres, that both the individuals and the marriage initials on these wares were usually those of the customer rather than the potter.

A mark which has been suggested as Flower's is a sprig, after the manner of the Chinese prunus blossom: it is supposed to be a rebus on Flower's name. It appears notably on a dish once in the Swann Collection which depicts 'Joshua commanding the sun to stand still'. But this device appears so universally on ceramics that here once again one seems to be faced with collectors' wishful thinking.

What appears to emerge from all this is that if these pieces have any connection at all with Flower, they offer no help in establishing either an individual artist's hand or even a general 'house' style. They could just as well be items left behind in the warehouse which were sold up when his niece 'M. Ewer' begged leave to inform her friends and the public 'that she has taken over the Stock in Trade of her late Uncle Mr Joseph Flower, and has laid in a fresh Assortment of Glass and Staffordshire Ware both useful and Ornamental'.

Ornamental vase in the Chinese style. Liverpool, c. *1750.* (Sotheby and Co.)

Liverpool tiles, transfer printed in black by Sadler and Green, with portraits of contemporary actors and actresses in character. c. *1778–80.* (Victoria and Albert Museum.)

A number of other Bristol delftware painters are known to us by name, but again attributions have been made to them on no very sure grounds. One very distinctive style which is found on a great deal of Bristol ware is awarded—on the evidence of one signed plate (p. 11) which has now disappeared—to John Bowen, who, as already noted, was an apprentice at the Limekiln Lane pottery under John Weaver. Bowen was the son of a Bristol watchmaker, and when Weaver had retired, his apprenticeship was transferred to Charles Christopher and again in 1749 to John Bundy. Pountney says that Bowen also worked for Flower, on what evidence one does not know.

There is hardly any mistaking the 'Bowen' style, if only for the highly individual way in which the foliage of the trees is dabbed in, apparently with a sponge. One ubiquitous pattern shows a river scene with a long building on the far shore and mountains beyond; there are sailing vessels or rowing-boats in the middle distance, and the larger the plates, the more vessels are shown. Somewhere in the picture there is usually a flight of birds in V-formation. The missing documentary plate together with the signature was illustrated in Hugh Owen's book *Two Centuries of Ceramic Art in Bristol* (1873), and both are reproduced here (p. 11).

Less convincing is the attribution to John Niglett of some *chinoiseries* with stylized Chinese figures, on the evidence of a plate bearing the initials J. N. E. and dated 1733. This seems to rest solely upon Pountney's discovery that the painter Niglett's wife was named Esther. Niglett was

apprenticed to Thomas Dixon at Brislington in 1714, but little else is known about him. Pountney says he also worked for Ward and Frank. His name appears in the Poll Book of 1754 as a potter in Redcliff.

A name well known to glass collectors is Michael Edkins, an interesting character who appears in another book in this series.[1] Edkins is said to have been a painter of delftware as well as glass, but only on the strength of a plate bearing initials (p. 11) which correspond to those of himself and his wife. It was claimed by his grandson to have been Edkins's own work, but this may have been only a family tradition.

(*c*) LIVERPOOL

Earliest of the Liverpool delftware factories seems to be that established by Alderman Thomas Shaw at Shaw's Brow, premises which were afterwards broken up among a number of different potters. From this establishment comes a large panel measuring 31 in. by 20 in. with a crudely painted landscape of Great Crosby. This is dated 1716, and is thus the earliest piece of authenticated Liverpool delft.

Richard Chaffers, an apprentice of Shaw's, was another maker of galleyware, and so also was Zachariah Barnes, a native of Warrington, born in 1743. He started business in the old Haymarket, and made druggists' jars and pots, dishes and plates, tiles, wine and spirit labels and also those small round charpots (p. 20) which were a speciality of the

[1] *All Kinds of Small Boxes*: John Bedford.

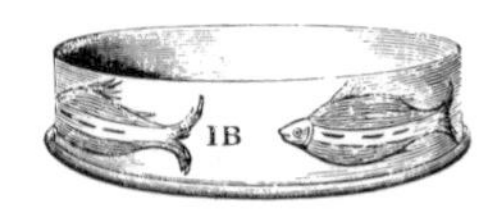

Charpot, wine-bin label, plaque and marriage mug in Liverpool delftware, eighteenth century.
(*Ceramic Art in Great Britain.*)

Liverpool potteries. He was one of the suppliers of tiles to the printers Sadler and Green (p. 18/19).

Chaffers had a distinguished name in Liverpool potting for his introduction there of the art of porcelain. He was almost the exact contemporary of Josiah Wedgwood and started in business on his own account in 1752. Much of his ware—as of most other Liverpool galleyware-makers—was made for export to America. Among these was a characteristic pepper pot inscribed with his name, and it appears that it was said at that time of an angry person that he was 'as hot as Dick's pepper pot'.

James, John and Seth Pennington, three brothers, all had potworks at which they made delftware, the last named building up an extensive business particularly noted for the large punch bowls characteristic of Liverpool (p. 35). They also made vases and beakers in the Chinese styles. Philip Christian had a galleyware-pottery on Shaw's Brow, at the corner of the street which was named after him.

Liverpool delftware shows a variety of tints: there is a clear bluish tone, also a dead white. One variety of delftware made there was so hard as almost to earn classification as stoneware. Much of the ware can be documented by a range of plates bearing names and places associated with the neighbourhood: the Mayor Collection at the Walker Gallery, Liverpool, gathered in the neighbourhood before dispersal of pieces among collectors farther afield, also helped in identification.

(*d*) GLASGOW

Delftfield Lane, Glasgow, near the Broomielaw, suggests itself as a centre of galleyware making—although, of course, 'Delft' could equally well indicate any kind of digging for clay (for example, at Lane Delph, in Staffordshire). There is, however, strong evidence that tin-glazed ware was made there from 1748 onwards by Robert Dinwoodie. A punch-bowl in the People's Palace Museum is painted in blue with the arms of the city; but in general little is known about the Glasgow productions.

(*e*) DUBLIN

Much more information is to be had about the wares made in the Irish centres, which are said to have included Dublin, Limerick, Rostrevor, Waterford and Wexford. Dublin wares are sometimes marked with the name of the town; for example, a plate in the Victoria and Albert Museum which is dated 1735 and bears the arms of the Earl of Dorset. It is thought to have been made by John Chapman, who was potting in Dublin at that date. A factory owned by John Crisp and Co. was possibly the same as that taken over in 1752 by Henry Delamain (*d.* 1757) and continued by his widow and others at least as late as 1771. A monogram of H and D is his mark, and there are also the initials 'N.E.', thought to be a painter's mark. There are close affinities between much of the Dublin work and that of Liverpool, but the Irish capital also favoured some of the shapes of the French faience which was being imported into Ireland—although they tended to decorate them in English rather than in Continental styles.

(*f*) LIMERICK

Of the other Irish potteries, only Limerick offers us any real documentation on wares. A pair of interesting plates from this town were shown to the English Ceramic Circle before the war, one of which bore the inscription in blue 'Made by John Strich, Limerick, 1761' while the other put the date in full '4 June 1761'. This John Strich, together with another potter named Christopher Bridson, was in 1762 awarded a premium of thirty pounds for 'erecting a manufactory of earthenware in imitation of delft or white ware'. There appears to be no other record of the two potters except for that of Strich's death in 1768.

The plates belong to two armorial services of the same pattern, one bearing the arms of Viscount Perry (1719–1806) and the other those of Francis Pierpoint Burton, M.P. for County Clare. The late Mr W. B. Honey, who introduced the plates to the Circle, conjectured that they might have been made by the potters for these obviously influential gentlemen to earn support for their claim for the above-mentioned premium.

The plates are $8\frac{5}{8}$ in. in diameter, the glaze has a bluish tone, and the edges are a strong brownish red. The tinctures of the arms are in blue, purplish black and dull yellow, while the flowers and foliage on the rim are touched with turquoise green and the same yellow. An interesting point about them is that they are transfer-printed from an engraving in (as Mr Honey described it) a soft purple brown overglaze line, the other colour being added by the brush. There is, in fact, reason to believe that there is a link here with the Battersea enamel factory, for Henry Delamain, the Dublin potter, as is known from the Battersea rate books, was a proprietor at York House, where the enamelling was carried on.

3. The Styles: 'Maiolica' and 'Delftware'

Before giving an account of the objects made in delftware, it may first be worth looking at the decorative styles used.

As was indicated early in our story, collectors today prefer the word maiolica to delftware for the first of the English galleywares. But in fact the very earliest surviving types of tin-glazed earthenware of undoubted English origin seem to owe their inspiration to quite a different source, namely the stoneware silver-mounted jugs with mottled glazes known as 'tiger ware', which in their turn were derived from the Rhenish stonewares being imported into the country.

These so-called 'Malling' jugs—after the church in Kent where one of them was found—have mounts with dates from 1549 until the seventeenth century, and are fine wares, with glazes in mottled dark blue and purple, turquoise, and also blue flecked with orange and other colours. The evidence now seems to suggest that they came from a lost London factory rather than Kent.

ELIZABETHAN POTTERS

Earliest of these, and seemingly the work of potters around Aldgate and St Katherine's Dock between say 1570 and 1600, is a range of drug jars, vases, jugs, etc. decorated with floral motifs and chevrons in blue, orange, green and purple. Some of them may, in fact, have been imported from the Netherlands, but there are shapes which have clearly been copied from English silverware; furthermore many have duller colours than one would expect from the Flemish ware. The earliest dated piece of undoubted English maiolica is a dish in the London Museum which bears the date 1600 and the charming inscription: 'THE ROSE IS RED THE LEAVES ARE GRENE GOD SAVE ELIZABETH OUR QUEENE'.

The first of the maiolica wares to acquire any kind of distinctive English style, however, are thought to have been made at Southwark by Christian Wilhelm. Typical of them is a barrel-shaped mug (p. 25) in the Victoria and Albert Museum, bearing the inscription 'Elizabeth Brocklehurst' and the date 1628 in a panel reserved on a ground of speckled purple.

Apart from these, there were other wares in pleasant colours, for example, a dish in the Fitzwilliam Museum with floral decoration in green, yellow, orange and purple. Another early style is shown in the starry flowers used on a mug which celebrates the marriage of William and Elizabeth Burges, in the Victoria and Albert Museum (p. 25). There is also an Italianate style in which the caryatids, sphinxes and birds of Urbino have been freely adapted, as on a mug (p. 25) once owned by 'Ann Chapman' and dated 1642.

The formal Ming styles of the reign of Wan Li were often seen in maiolica. There were mugs painted in blue monochrome with Chinese motifs of birds, insects and rocks which perhaps represent the first appearance in English ceramics of themes which were to fascinate the porcelain makers of Chelsea and Bow more than a century later.

There were also other foreign influences making themselves felt. From France came a taste for the relief dishes made in glazed earthenware by Bernard Palissy, especially the famous 'La Fécondité', showing a nude woman with her children. There are others with reptiles, shells and plants, and some of these are in colour, others in blue monochrome. Also from France came a very attractive form of decoration using a dark blue enamel ground with designs painted in opaque white (p. 26). It was developed at Nevers, in imitation of the *bleu persan* of the Middle East, and is now known as *bleu de Nevers*. Plates, jugs, mugs and other items were given this decoration, sometimes in simple splashes of white enamel, sometimes with fine outline drawing of flowers or Chinamen.

NATURE THEMES

During the eighteenth century many styles and themes ran

concurrently with each other and there was considerable cross-fertilization between different crafts, for silver, porcelain, delftware and other earthenwares were often made quite near each other and were even sold in the same shop.

At Limekiln Lane, Bristol, a bird and tree pattern was popular, also groups showing a church and a basket of fruit. Another very English design shows a fox jumping over a blue mound. The pleasant 'Farmhouse' groups of birds—peacocks, gamecocks, hawks and pheasants in bright polychrome (p. 27) were probably also made at Limekiln Lane.

CHINOISERIES

The Wan Li themes first seen in the seventeenth century were followed by true *chinoiserie*, that is to say, a European romanticization of Chinese themes and subjects, but now taken from the contemporary K'ang Hsi and Ch'ien Lung wares. The Lambeth work in this field was often more attractive than the original. The 'rat and vine' motif shows a squirrel among grape and vine leaves; then there was the 'Jumping Chinaman' and the 'Chinaman among grasses' (p. 26), the so-called 'Long Elizas', the tall

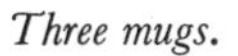

Three mugs.
(Left) *Inscribed 'Elizabeth Brocklehurst, 1628', in mottled cobalt blue and purple, perhaps made by Christian Wilhelm at Southwark.*
(Centre) *Inscribed 'Ann Chapman' painted in colours, with 'Urbino grotesques'. London, dated 1642.*
(Right) *Inscribed 'William and Elizabeth Burges, 24th August, 1632', painted in colours. Probably Southwark.*
(All Victoria and Albert Museum.)

slender oriental ladies whom the Dutch traders called *lange lijsen* (literally maypoles), and, of course, the familiar prunus blossom and 'cracked ice' themes of the breaking-up of the winter and the coming of the spring. Bright reds, greens, yellows and blues now appear, with imitations of the *famille verte* porcelains in their dominating green.

Coloured grounds came into fashion, mainly in powder blue and purple, but also in light blue-green and sometimes in the rarer 'dead-leaf' brown. White panels were reserved in the grounds by placing pieces of paper on the areas intended for decoration. After covering the rest of the ground with glaze the paper was removed and the panels were painted. There are marked differences in the handling of all these motifs and subjects, and collectors find these useful in dating and attributing them to the various centres.

'BIANCO SOPRA BIANCO'

'White on white'—which is what *bianco sopra bianco* means literally—is an odd description of a process in which applied white slip decoration is placed over a coloured ground, usually blue. It is based upon Italian maiolica originals, which themselves had white decoration on either white or tinted plates, in the style of some incised Chinese work. But this hardly explains why we did not instead adopt another

(Left) *Election plate. Bristol, 1754.*
(Centre) '*Merryman*' *plate. London,* c. *1680* (see p. 39).
(Right) '*Farmyard*' *plate, showing a pheasant in polychrome colours. Bristol, eighteenth century.*
(All Sotheby and Co.)

ready-made and more accurately descriptive term *bianco sopra azzurro.*

Despite this the decoration has produced some of the most attractive English delftware. It was used at all three main centres, and also in Sweden at Rorstrand and in France at St Amand-les-Eaux; but there are marked differences in the way it was used at all the centres. There are several patterns even on the English wares, with variations in the management of the leaf-sprays of the flowers or pineapples.

Bianco is at its most delightful when in combination with brilliant polychrome motifs nicely placed in the centre of the plates. It is also to be found associated with all the motifs and styles attributed, rightly or wrongly, to Joseph Flower and John Bowen, especially the latter. It appears sometimes on Liverpool pieces painted in the brilliant, so-called 'Fazackerly' colours which show polychrome flowers in a variety of designs, using purple, blue, a foxy red, green and yellow (colour plate). The same colours are sometimes used for other themes. They derive the name from two mugs made for a local couple named Thomas and Catherine Fazackerly, bearing initials and dates.

Overglaze painting in the Dutch manner (colour plate) is rarely seen on English delftware, and, to judge by the decorative themes used, it appears to have been done mainly at Liverpool.

.ambeth bleeding bowl and mug, howing two different styles of bleu de Nevers. c. *1680–90* (p. 24). (Sotheby .nd Co.)

Blue dash chargers

Charles II, London
(Sotheby and Co.)

William and Mary
(Sotheby and Co.)

William IV
(Sotheby and Co.)

George I
(Sotheby and Co.)

Adam and Eve
(Victoria and Albert Museum.)

Family group—a marriage plate, 1614
(Victoria and Albert Museum.)

4. The Wares

(*a*) BLUE-DASH CHARGERS

When the late Father Downman awarded this name to a well-known class of delftware dishes and plates it did not worry him—nor need it us—that many of them were not really large enough to be called chargers, that they did not necessarily have the characteristic painted 'dashes' round the rim, and that the 'dashes' were not always blue. But the name has been universally adopted for a recognizable type which has always fascinated collectors, and today these pieces command respectable and even sometimes sensational prices in the auction rooms. A few years ago an Adam and Eve charger of the 1630s put up to auction at Sotheby's made no less than 840 guineas.

Blue-dash chargers range in diameter from 8½ in. to 16½ in. but average about 13¼ in.; and they are decorated mainly in the spectacular high-temperature colours developed by late Stuart times. They were made, not so much for use on the table, but to stand on shelf or court cupboard, also to be hung on walls. There is usually a rim base capable of taking a string or wire, with sometimes a hole for a wooden peg: the collector need not be concerned if he finds that this hole is in many cases so placed that if one suspended the plate from it the picture would hang askew. Like the Italian and Netherlands maiolica dishes on which many of them were modelled, they provided a family picture gallery in an age when easel pictures were rare and expensive.

There are some who hold that the blue 'dashes' are a cruder version of an older 'rope' pattern; others that they have links with the gadrooned edges of pewter and silver dishes or the nicked edges of the old combed slipware baking pans, as seen in pastry. The 'dashes' are sometimes in red or green; alternatively there may be a 'sponge' or other border, or perhaps none at all. Some have a wide flat rim like the contemporary pewter plate, others a very narrow raised edge, perhaps with a kind of embossing produced simply by the potter's poking his finger into the wet clay.

SUBJECT PAINTING

For subjects, the chargers show biblical scenes, family groups, portraits of royal and other distinguished persons, and patterns made up of flowers, fruit and foliage. Mr Robert Hall Warren told the English Ceramic Circle some years ago that he had come across some 750 chargers in his time, of which no fewer than 170 represented the Fall, showing Adam and Eve in the Garden of Eden on either side of the tree round which the serpent was coiled (p. 28). There are others depicting the Return of the Prodigal Son, Mary Magdalene, the Nativity, the Walk to Emmaus, Abraham Sacrificing Isaac, Jacob's Dream, etc.

Mr Warren's figures are interesting in the light they shed on the relative popularity of the public personages whose portraits appear on chargers. Altogether 150 were decorated in this way, and these were made up as follows: one of Edward VI, two of Charles II, four of James II, sixty of William III, twenty of the latter with his consort Mary II, five of Mary II on her own, thirty of Queen Anne, ten of George I, and three of George II. (See p. 28.) No monarchs since seem to have been commemorated in this way.

Quite often the same picture is used for different persons, one set of initials being substituted for another—for example, when D.M. is used it stands for the Duke of Marlborough, P.E. for Prince Eugene, P.G. for Prince George of Denmark (Queen Anne's husband), and D.O. for the Duke of Ormond. Many of the chargers bear dates and also the familiar triple initials of married couples which, incidentally, rarely seem to appear on anything but English pottery.

Pill slab, with the arms of the Society of Apothecaries of London, eighteenth century. (Sotheby and Co.)

Nobody can pretend, I think, that these subject chargers are great works of art. Compared with the work of the great Italian masters of maiolica painting they must rank as peasant art, like much of the Dutch work of the earlier period. All the same their very artlessness has its appeal—as it does in the work done in Staffordshire somewhat later on salt-glazed stoneware and creamware.

'TULIP' CHARGERS

About the tulip and other floral designs on these chargers, however, it is difficult not to be unreservedly lyrical (colour plate). In the seventeenth century there was wild enthusiasm and enormous financial speculation in tulip growing and fancying, especially in Holland, and one supposes that the English potters picked up the general idea from that country. But the rendering is as free and vigorous and totally native as the painting which was to appear on the Staffordshire stoneware already mentioned—and suggests, incidentally, that many delftware painters from Lambeth and Bristol must have migrated to Staffordshire in the 1720s and 1730s when these new wares were emerging.

Some of these patterns, especially those using irises and fritillaries, are strongly reminiscent of some kinds of Turkish pottery, notably the so-called 'Rhodian' ware from Isnik. One wonders if this was taken direct rather than through the Low Countries. There are also some fine examples of the 'bursting pomegranate' patterns which the Flemings took from Venice and passed on both to England and Delft; sometimes these 'fruit' designs are stylized almost into geometry.

That Lambeth were prolific makers of these wares is shown in various ways, notably the discovery of fragments near the site of Doulton's pottery. Bristol were also concerned with them in the early days, but Liverpool, Wincanton and the Irish factories seem to have come in only at the end of the period.

Wine bottle. London, 1647
(Sotheby and Co.)

(*b*) WINE BOTTLES

The Englishness of English delftwares, and the charm they oppose to the highly sophisticated wares of the Dutch and the Italians, is nowhere better seen than in the race of wine bottles. Historically, they stand between the German stoneware Bellarmines, on which they seem to have been modelled, and the dark-green glass 'dumpy' bottles, stuck with seals bearing their owners' initials or crests, which eventually superseded them.

These admirable little pot-bellied shapes are usually covered with the finest of white tin-glaze, which needs—and usually gets—no more decoration than the odd flourish around an owner's initials, the date and a short description of the content—Sack, Claret, Whit, Boy and the rest.

Of these, 'sack' is perhaps the most often seen. The term, which one meets everywhere in literature—especially when characters like Sir John Falstaff are about—was once thought to have indicated a dry type of sherry, after the words *sec* or *seco*. But it has since been very convincingly argued by Mr H. Warner Allen in his inestimable *History of Wine* that the shippers of Jerez—whence came our 'Sherries'—referred to them by the word *sac* (from the Spanish verb *sacar*, to take out) as denoting exported goods. Thus 'sack' seems to have meant export sherry. The term 'Whit' means, one supposes, white wine, although it is odd that it should be so consistently mis-spelt. 'Boy' also puzzles: these jugs are surely too early to have picked up the slang term 'The Boy' which later writers used of Champagne—though this beverage was in fact known to the Restoration Court.

As with the amphoræ of the ancient Greeks, many of these bottles have a grooved neck, so that they may have a parchment or some other sealing material tied around their necks. Their small size in an age when drinking capacities were enormous—they were usually only 6 or 7 in. high and could scarcely hold more than half a pint—has led some commentators to wonder if they were not used for clients' samples of particular consignments or vintages. But sack was surely not offered in vintages at that date nor transported in such small quantities, and one inclines to the view put forward by Professor Garner that they are a seventeenth-century version of the 'gift-pack' bottle one sees offered today in the shops at Christmas time. The bottles often bear dates; and Pepys and other writers have recorded the fact that they were given bottles of sack on New Year's Day. By the same reasoning, specimens bearing the familiar triangularly placed trio of initials could have been wedding presents.

Sometimes the bottles have such wide necks as to be thought of as jugs or early 'decantors': they may also have lugs or ears, after the manner of pilgrim bottles or gourds. Some have the front of the neck pinched in to form a spout for easy pouring; and perhaps a transition to the short cylindrical glass bottle which superseded them is marked in one decorated with *chinoiseries* which is illustrated by Mr Geoffrey Eliot Howard in the book mentioned on p. 42. The globular ones seem to have been produced over a relatively short period, for their known dates range only from 1629 to 1672.

A *caveat* to collectors: some quite genuine but undecorated wine bottles—and also other Stuart and Georgian vessels—have within the last century

Fuddling cup. London, late seventeenth century. (Victoria and Albert Museum.)

John Udy of Luxillion
his tin was so fine
it gliderd this punch bowl
and made it to Shine
pray fill it with punch
lett the tinners sitt round
they never will budge
till the bottom they found
1731

Inscription from a punchbowl, addressed by the delftware makers to their supplier of tin. John Udy of Luxillion, Cornwall, 1731. (Victoria and Albert Museum.)

been given decoration (some say in the Netherlands and France) to increase their interest for collectors; but the sharp informed eye will note some palpable inconsistencies in these additions.

(*c*) PUNCH-BOWLS

Like their counterparts in other wares, punch-bowls form one of the most splendid and important classes of English delftware.

Most comfortably off families had their punch-bowls, which they brought out on important occasions and filled with the hot steaming punch in which the eighteenth century delighted. Hosts vied with each other in devising their own special brews.

Occupying so conspicuous a place in the household affairs, it was no wonder that fine workmanship should be put into them. This is especially true of the famous Liverpool ship bowls. One important specimen wishes 'Success to the Monmouth' and shows a picture of the ship herself. Characteristic Liverpool bowls also have paintings of weapons and naval equipment on the outside, sometimes in the 'Fazackerly' colours (colour plate).

Bristol made a well-known punch-bowl which shows a family on its way to church, the thirteen children all being carefully graduated in size. But the West Country port also had its ship bowls, and like the potters on Merseyside, made a speciality of supplying bowls to ships visiting the port. The Manchester City Art Gallery has one which bears an inscription in (inaccurate) Swedish commemorating the docking of a ship at Bristol in 1765: similar ones are known in Sweden itself, while there is one Liverpool ship bowl with an inscription in Dutch. *Bianco sopra bianco* (colour plate) was used on some of these bowls.

Political slogans abound on punch-bowls, also mock coats-of-arms with ribald verses. Some long-departed sheep-master is remembered on a bowl with a pastoral landscape and a vine border in the British Museum which is inscribed 'Richard Wyatt, Appellsham. Prosperity to the Flock. May 30th 1754'.

There are differences to be noted in the forms of the bowls. The earlier ones seem to be deeper than those made later, and also have higher footrims. Bristol specimens have more rounded sides, and some of the Liverpool ones are exceptionally large.

(*d*) DRINKING VESSELS

A small but rewarding section of collecting lies in the many varied cups, beakers, tankards, mugs and the like which were made in delftware.

There is, to start with, the simple 'cup' with a single handle (p. 37), which perhaps once had a saucer. But there is the 'cup' without a handle which has been called a wine cup, and the 'cup' which is also a goblet (p. 44), though it may well have done duty as a communion cup. One finds mugs, sometimes with no handles, and more splendid affairs which surely earn the right to be called tankards (p. 37).

Two views of a Liverpool ship bowl.

Many of these early drinking vessels are painted with a royal portrait and a date, or they may have the owner's name and a coat-of-arms; others are inscribed with the names of livery companies such as the Carpenters, the Leathersellers, etc. Historical occasions are sometimes marked; for example a globular cup with a high neck is inscribed 'God sen ye King save to Irland'—apparently a contemporary reference to King William III and the Battle of the Boyne. The vigorous and sometimes bawdy humour of the day is shown in such items as a cup showing a man wearing the horns and holding a goblet: beside this is the age-old gibe: 'O I was born to wear the horns'. Some unkind person has rammed the joke home here by adding a set of initials: one wonders why the recipient allowed it to survive.

Some of these early cups are in monochrome blue, others have purple and yellow; but greater variety of decoration is seen in the mugs and tankards. Pretty mugs in the first of the English maiolica styles are shown on p. 25, but, as mug grows into tankard, one sees echoes of silver, pewter and stoneware. There is the early barrel shape, with its rings, and then the globe with the high neck, bearing dates of about 1650–60. This was perhaps taken direct from the red stoneware of the Netherlands, of Dwight of Fulham or the Dutch Elers brothers in Staffordshire: a tradition continued in the later stonewares of Chesterfield and Derby. The two ceramic materials would have been in direct competition.

Mugs or tankards may have delicately drawn and brightly coloured birds, taken from Chinese themes, notably at Lambeth; or they may bear cruder designs not unlike those seen on Staffordshire lustre wares. The *bleu persan* treatment (colour plate and p. 26) also occurs on mugs from Lambeth. Straight sides and fillets round the base, with outward flaring foot, take the story on; and by the middle of the century Liverpool especially seems to have favoured the bell or ogee shape.

Some Lambeth mugs have the bottom made of glass from

the near-by Vauxhall factory, like those seen in pewter during the nineteenth century.

Puzzle jugs are to be found in delftware as in most other forms of pottery. Here, as is well known, it is a matter of stopping up certain of the holes and sucking vigorously at one of them, usually one coming up inside the handle. A type inscribed with crudish verses hails from Liverpool; there is also the well known

Here, gentlemen, come try your skill,
I'll hold a wager if you will
That you can't drink this liquor all
Without you spill and let some fall.

The perforations on the necks of the Liverpool jugs tend to consist of four hearts arranged in a circle, sometimes with ellipses between. At Bristol, however, the necks are perforated by intersecting circles. Lambeth also produced its puzzle jugs, but seems to have preferred a type with much narrower necks—perhaps being earlier in date they followed the stoneware types more closely.

Another member of this jape and joke family is the attractive looking little fuddling cup (p. 33), which is actually a combination of three or four cups joined together not only externally but internally; so that in trying to empty one of them—not an insuperable task—you have to drain all three. The earliest recorded date on one of these is 1633.

(Top) *Lambeth mug, bearing the arms of the Watermens' Company, 1682.*
(Centre) *Mug with inscription, 1785.*
(Bottom) *Puzzle jug. Lambeth, 1742.*
(All Sotheby and Co.)

(Left to right) *Plate with scalloped edge, dated 1683. Salt, London,* c. *1650. Porringer with marriage initials from dinner set, 1686.* (Sotheby and Co.)

(*e*) TABLE WARES

Wooden platters were followed by pewter plates: and after pewter—although for many years alongside it—delftware. Many an old house has shelves and rails which its owners still call the 'delft-rack'. Here were kept the plates and dishes bought by those envious of the fine porcelains of China but finding them rather heavy on the purse.

Differences of style in these 'useful' wares will often be helpful in dating and attributing to one or other of the centres. The earliest plates all had flat bottoms, as in pewter, with, however, sides turning up at a very shallow angle. But at Bristol the typical shape from early eighteenth century to about 1770 had a flat bottom with sides at a sharper angle. Later types again tended to be thicker and heavier.

At Lambeth, however, what would in pewter be called the 'booge' was curved up to a flat everted rim. From about 1730 onwards all the centres adopted the Chinese form of plate with a raised footrim alongside their other shapes. The raised footrim usually went with the more elaborate type of decoration.

Decorative styles are dealt with elsewhere, but there are several types of plates which should be mentioned here. Of great rarity now in full sets, though often to be seen in incomplete ones, are the famous 'Merryman' plates (p. 27), each of which bears a single line of these verses:

> What is a Merry Man?
> Let him doo what he cann
> To entertain his guest
> With Wine and Merry Jest
> But if his Wife does Frown
> All merriment goes down.

The lettering of these inscriptions has sometimes been taken as an indication of Netherlanders working in London. Spelling, of course, was nobody's strong suit in the seventeenth and eighteenth centuries, even among the educated, but one wonders on seeing 'do what hee Kan', which appears on some of them, if an Englishman would misspell in quite that way. When a set turns up in the salerooms it attracts a good price. In 1962, at Sotheby's, Mr R. C. Arbuthnot sold a superb set which had been in his family since it was potted: it made the handsome sum of £1,200.

Election plates (p. 27) were made in numbers everywhere and especially at Bristol, Wincanton and Liverpool. Affairs of public interest were commemorated: for instance the case of Dr Henry Sacheverell, who was arraigned for seditious sermonizing, but was afterwards vindicated and made a national hero. Admirals Keppel and Ross had their plates, as also did that King of Prussia, Frederick the Great, whom we supported in the Seven Years' War and so made an English hero.

Few Jacobite inscriptions appear on plates, but there is one inscribed 'No Pretender'. The balloon ascent of Lunardi in 1783 took place only a few

Foodwarmer, eighteenth century.
(Sotheby and Co.)

hundred yards from the Lambeth works, so naturally enough it is shown on a good many plates made there.

Lambeth also made four- and five-lobed dishes described as trinket or sweetmeat trays; there are others where five or more inner dishes fit inside a larger one, as in creamware types. Some dishes, to judge by similar forms in china, may well be teapot stands and spoon trays. Although delftware did not take all that kindly to boiling water, there are teacups and saucers and quite a number of teapots (p. 40) with pleasant *chinoiserie* and other painting.

(*f*) APOTHECARIES' JARS

Medical men and institutions collect delftware pharmacy or apothecary jars with such enthusiasm that it is a wonder there are any left for the lay collector. But they do appear quite frequently at sales and in the shops, and rarely lack a buyer.

The English jars (p. 41) are quite unlike those in maiolica (p. 48): here is no splendid *istoriato* painting nor flowing arabesques, but usually only the abbreviated forms of the drugs they contained, together with some perfunctory scroll work and perhaps surmounted by an angel or some other figure.

The inscriptions on them take us back into a world of dusty shelves in long-vanished apothecaries' shops. There

Teapot. Lambeth, c. *1750.* (Ceylon Tea Centre.)

Drug or apothecaries' jars. London, late seventeenth and early eighteenth centuries. (Royal College of Surgeons of England.)

was S.E.SUCC.ROS, a syrup made from roses which was said to 'strengthen the heart, comfort the spirit, build the body, help fluxes, and corrosion and gnawing of the guts, and stay vomiting'. E.MITHRIDAT was the electuary Mithridates, which was once regarded as a universal antidote to poisons and originally contained no fewer than fifty-four ingredients. LOH. Sanv. & Ex. signals for us a thick syrupy concoction prepared from pine kernels, almonds, poppy-heads, liquorice and orris roots.

Jars intended for dry drugs usually had the albarello shape, not in the waisted versions of Italy and Spain (p. 48), but with the rounded and footed styles of German Kreussen faience and Roeren stoneware—no doubt the form was copied from the early Netherlands potteries. For wet drugs they were usually more or less globular, mounted upon a spreading foot, and equipped with a spout and sometimes also a handle. Some appear to have had covers once, perhaps of pewter; others may have been designed for sealing with a wooden stopper or a piece of parchment.

Most of the English jars are decorated in plain blue on a white ground which sometimes has a pinky tone. By comparing dated specimens, of which there are many, it has been possible to group them according to styles. Those with dates which can point only to Lambeth manufacture usually have a grotesque head at either end of the panel containing the name of the drug; this is perhaps an echo of Urbino, or some other Italian factory, and it was popular about the time of the Commonwealth.

Barbers' bowl, with a segment cut to fit the neck and showing implements of the trade. London, 1706. (Sotheby and Co.)

But *chinoiserie* also appears on jars of this time—one is dated 1658 and also bears the arms of the Apothecaries' Company. This device is to be found on the pill slab shown on p. 30; the motto *opiferque per orbem dicor* comes from Ovid's story of Apollo and Daphne, where Apollo reassures the nymph that the art of medicine is his discovery. 'I am called help-bringer throughout the world,' he says, 'and all potency of herbs is given to me.'

It has been suggested that the larger jars which also bore the Company's arms but without the name of a drug were made to stand in windows and proclaim the apothecary's membership of his professional body—much as does today the plaque of the British Antique Dealers' Association.

Returning to the drug jars, another style in vogue during the last third of the seventeenth century shows the end of the panel twisted downwards in a scrolled ribbon with detached ends.

Somewhere about 1650 appears the first of the 'angel' type jars, whereon an angel is shown above the panel, its wings spreading out on either side. The 'angel' may sometimes be wearing horns, and later the contemporary wig which at last blossoms out into the full-bottomed periwig. Mr G. E. Howard, in his *Early English Drug Jars*, has worked out many of these classifications, and claims to have discovered sufficient similarities in the styles of these various 'angels' to be able to trace them to different artists whose names remain unknown.

The Jacobean jars were succeeded by a much more professional-looking type; and here Mr Howard proposes two more classes, the 'Birds' and the 'Cherubs'. They are much more common on Dutch jars, and probably originated there—although the cherubs' heads are also to be found in this country on memorial tablets of the era. Were the apothecaries anticipating the worst?

Interesting collections of these jars have been built up by some of the professional bodies having links with the old apothecaries and pharmacists. The Royal College of Surgeons of England has a representative gathering not only of English (p. 41) and Dutch jars, but also of fine specimens in Italian maiolica and nineteenth-century French faience; the Wellcome Foundation also includes them in its collection of medical bygones; and the Society of Apothecaries of London has a fine selection of Continental types.

(*g*) PORRINGERS, POSSET POTS AND CAUDLE CUPS

With these items, delftware takes us deep into the manners and customs of late Stuart and Georgian England.

Porringers are bowls with two flat handles sticking out like ears. (They are also made in pewter and silver.) The word porringer here is probably derived from 'porage', i.e. soup, rather than porridge: perhaps we should call them broth bowls.

Posset pots and caudle cups are two-handled pots with a lid and spout—in the earliest records they are described as 'spout pots'—and they range from types as attractively simple as the wine bottles already described to elaborately decorated affairs, sometimes surmounted by a crown or a figure.

Posset was primarily a hot drink in which milk or cream was curdled with ale, wine or some other liquor, and then spiced and sweetened. Making it became an

Bristol polychrome 'brick' painted in famille rose *colours with European figures and jardiniers.* $5\frac{3}{4}$ *in. long.* (Christie's.)

Wall pocket. Lambeth, c. *1680.*

Money box, with initia[ls,] dated 1692.

Cat flower holder.

Flower vase. Lambeth, c. *1680.*

Pair of shoes. Lambeth, dated 1688.

Goblet, inscribed 'Mary Butler'.

Candlestick.

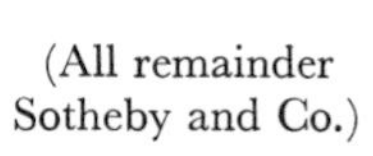

(All remainder Sotheby and Co.)

accomplishment, and drinking it a social occasion. Caudle, on the other hand, was a mixture of oatmeal or crushed biscuits with egg-yolk, wine or ale, and was either sweetened or spiced. It was given to invalids, especially women in child-birth: also, oddly enough, it appears to have been offered to those who called at the house after the birth of the child.

Some versions have no spout, and most authorities seem to believe that both types were used indiscriminately for posset or caudle. But I have often wondered, in view of the difficulties likely to be met with in sucking the thick caudle up through such a very thin spout, whether in fact the spout pots might not have been for posset and the spoutless two-handled cups with cover and stand for caudle, eaten with a spoon.

The earliest known posset pot is a straight-sided one in the Fitzwilliam Museum which bears the name of its owner Stephen Gardner and the date 1631. As one would expect from the date it belongs decoratively to English maiolica rather than delftware. From about 1670 onwards a shape with double curved sides became fashionable, and it was in the last third of the century that they appeared with fantastic decoration often surmounted by a crown, a cross or figure of some kind. Such large and elaborate affairs seem to suggest presentation pieces, and they do often bear initials of owners and dates, like those in porcelain and silver. A glass version is shown in a forthcoming book in this series.[1]

(*h*) ORNAMENTAL AND ODD

Delftware flourished in an age when makers of china and earthenware everywhere liked to break away from the 'useful' wares which were their bread and butter and offer their customers more ornamental or diverting pieces.

Liverpool, as already noted, was a producer of the large *potiche* (p. 17) and the trumpet-mouthed beaker which made up the *garniture de cheminée* of three or five pieces

[1] *English Crystal Glass*: John Bedford.

familiar in Chinese and Continental porcelain. In general, however, England did not attempt to rival the Netherlands in this field. A type of flower vase which stands on a pedestal and has three projecting spouts for flowers is a smaller version of the sometimes huge affairs found in Dutch delft (p. 57).

There are also rectangular boxes called 'bricks' (p. 44), used either as inkstands or vases, their tops being perforated with large and small holes. They come in a variety of styles: some Bristol bricks have square holes, and a curve is cut across the base leaving 'feet' at the corners, as in a bureau. Liverpool bricks may be scalloped out in a series of curves, or have a wash of blue over the top. There are Lambeth bricks which are straight-bottomed. Those designed as inkstands would presumably once have had an inkwell, the smaller holes being for quills resting in the lead shot which acted as a cleaner.

Candlesticks follow the forms, sometimes very delightfully (p. 44), of silver and pewter, and those in the plain white tin-glaze must be placed in the same class of wares as the wine bottles. But there are also elaborately decorated versions showing the styles of later times. Hand-warmers in the form of small prayer-books or shoes may originally have been containers of something, or were perhaps fitted as pincushions or snuffboxes.

Bleeding bowls, for letting blood from invalids, are apparently distinguished from porringers by having only one handle (p. 26). Those from Bristol and early Lambeth usually have a round hole and a scalloped or gadrooned outline: later Lambeth varieties may have holes in the shape of hearts or crosses.

Wall pockets for flowers (p. 44) are very collectable pieces for the decorator, coming as they do in a variety of shapes and styles. A great many of them originated in Liverpool, where the potters favoured the cornucopia, or horn of plenty, so often seen in other types of pottery. They may have relief moulding, particularly showing an angel head, with painted birds, flowers or fish: such pieces offer a rare glimpse of the rococo note in English delftware. There are others from Lambeth, however, with simple elliptical shapes and restrained decoration which perhaps anticipate the neo-classical styles—although, generally speaking, they seem to have come too late for delftware.

The galleyware-makers were not very adept hands at modelling figures. Hardly a trace is to be seen here of the native wit shown by Staffordshire men in their salt-glazed stoneware and lead-glazed earthenware—as shown in another book in this series.[1] Nor were the Dutch much better at this, as we shall presently see.

What human figures were made were usually rather crude copies from things in other wares, but there are birds and especially cats which have some charm (p. 44), though it usually rests in the decoration rather than the modelling. There are also owl figures, sometimes in undecorated white, sometimes perching on a rock.

Trinket boxes are to be found in delftware; also so-called trinket trays which may, however, be teapot stands or spoon trays.

TILES

English delftware tiles, though offering nothing like the range of the Dutch, have qualities of their own which make them good collecting.

The Bristol potteries favoured tiles in blue and purple monochromes (pp. 14/15), showing perhaps, baskets of flowers in the Dutch manner, birds, human figures, *chinoiserie*, or landscapes: there are in particular the fine polychrome birds attributed, like so many other good things, to Joseph Flower. Where foreign themes are used they usually have characteristic original touches.

Perhaps the most attractive of the painted tiles are those in *bianco sopra bianco* with birds or some other motif in polychrome. But there is a pleasing class which sets tiny

[1] *Staffordshire Pottery Figures*: John Bedford.

chinoiseries in the centre of a tile with borders in reserve. The 'John Bowen' style is also to be found here (p. 12).

Transfer printing appears on delftware; well known examples are some Liverpool tiles (pp. 18/19) printed by Sadler and Green, famous for their work on creamware. (An account of the process is given in another book in this series.[1]) They put out a whole series depicting stage personages of the day, also engravings of the type used on porcelain and creamware.

Panels are to be found, like the specimen for a mantelpiece, painted in blue with a view of a so far unidentified port, which may be seen in the Victoria and Albert Museum. It seems also to have been customary to mark a birth or some other domestic event by ordering from the galleyware-makers a slab or plaque painted with a name and a date.

Netherlandish maiolica dry-drug jar in albarello form. Antwerp, 1520–30. (Victoria and Albert Museum.)

[1] *All Kinds of Small Boxes*: John Bedford.

Dutch Delft

For the beginnings of tin-glazed earthenware in the Low Countries, one has to look not to Delft, but to Antwerp and towns of the Northern Netherlands, especially Haarlem, Rotterdam, Amsterdam and Middleburg. First of the *geleyerspotbakkers*, or galleypot-makers, to be recorded there was that Guido Andries, mentioned earlier, who is believed to be the same person as Guido da Savino, the Castel Durante maiolica maker who had emigrated to Antwerp and whose son or grandson came to Lambeth. Two tile pavements attributed to him have affinities of design with drug jars now in the Victoria and Albert Museum.

'NETHERLANDS MAIOLICA'

Styles and motifs used in these early days were, as one might suppose, heavily influenced by the Italian centres which were sending their wares round the Narrow Seas by galley. Here one sees the ripe bursting pomegranates, the grapes, and other exotic fruits then novel and so attractive to the northern palate. They were often given characteristically Netherlands borders, some of which found their way on to Lambeth ware: perhaps it was the 'rope' border of this era which set us off on 'blue-dash' chargers (p. 28).

A very different style, taken from the engravings of the day, showing strapwork, volutes and scrolls in imitation of ironwork, has been called *ferronerie*: and some very fine and delicate painting went into it. The misleadingly-named 'Delft-Urbino' style—it owes as much to Antwerp as to Delft—has grotesque figures in one of the Urbino modes, often with shields of arms and small landscapes, or subjects such as the Nativity.

'ISTORIATO' PAINTING

The *istoriato* painting which developed on Italian maiolica in imitation of easel pictures, many of the subjects being

Delft noir *dish, early eighteenth century.* (Rijksmuseum, Amsterdam.)

taken from Marcantonio Raimondi engravings, also appeared in the Netherlands. This style has been criticized as 'non-ceramic' in the way that it spread the subject arbitrarily over the rim and bowl of the plate or allowed perspective to dig a 'hole' in the middle of the piece. In defence of these works one might propose that they were, in fact, regarded as pictures rather than eating utensils. They do at least preserve for us the full magnificence of Renaissance colour, which on canvas is so often muted by time. Our own 'John Bowen' style, of course—if one may mention it in such august company as the work of great maiolica painters like Nicola Pellipario or Jacomo of Pesaro —spreads over the plate in precisely the same way.

CHINESE INFLUENCES

In the first half of the seventeenth century, the maiolica styles and themes lingered on in tiles (p. 63), especially at Rotterdam, and as we have seen they were followed at Lambeth and Bristol. But Chinese porcelain had now begun to flow into the Netherlands: it first appeared there in 1602, the result of looting a Portuguese ship. At first the styles seen were of late Ming times, mainly from the reign of Wan Li, and this was much used by the Dutch genre painters. Later, from about 1670, there came a great deal of K'ang Hsi blue and white. Slowly the maiolica makers found it necessary to meet this competition, either by imitating it or by offering native themes and subjects in its stead. It was in this mood that there arose the great faience-making centre of Delft.

THE RISE OF DELFT

In the early seventeenth century, the town of Delft was chiefly renowned for its excellent beer. There were nearly two hundred breweries in the town, whose maltsters sent their brews far and wide throughout Europe. But in the general upsurge of trade which followed the Treaty of Breda in 1609—whereby the Dutch threw off the Spanish yoke and established their new Republic—the brewers of Delft seem to have been overtaken by competitors in other towns. All through the first half of the century, one after another of them closed down until there were only fifteen left—presumably just enough to supply the thirst of the town itself.

Almost at once, however, the capital and energy thus released—and even more the buildings which had been occupied by the brewers—were taken up by a pottery industry quick to respond to the demands of the newly prosperous burghers, who wanted fine wares to show off in their houses. Delft was not particularly well supplied with potting materials—the local clays had to be blended with others from as far away as the Ruhr and England—but it was on a highway of international trade and already the home of a great race of painters and craftsmen in other fields. There were also all those empty breweries. To this last factor,

Roundel with landscape painted in blue by Frederik van Frijtom of Delft. 14½ in. in diameter, c. *1670.* (Victoria and Albert Museum.)

no doubt, we owe many of the colourful names by which the potteries are known—'The Metal Pot', 'The Double Jug', 'The Old Moor's Head' and the like.

As Guido Andries was the first recorded maiolica maker at Antwerp so another 'stranger' was the first known maker of tin-glazed earthenware at Delft. His name was Harman Pietersz. (the 'z' is shorthand for 'zoon' or son). He came to Delft from Haarlem in 1584, and was swiftly followed by potters from Antwerp and perhaps Rouen. The Guild of St Luke, of which Harman was a founder member, started in 1611 as an association for painters and sculptors, embroiderers, stainers of glass and so on, and slowly it opened its doors wider and wider to the makers of *Delfts porseleyn*—as in all the pride of self-advertisement the galleypot makers were now beginning to call their wares. They also described themselves as *plateelbakkers*, or dish-makers as distinct from *tegelbakkers*, or makers of tiles.

DUTCH ORIENTAL 'BLUE AND WHITE'

The competition from the Far East was met in two ways. The earliest class of wares imitated the fine monochromes decorated in the cobalt blue which the Ming potters had found to be the most practical pigment for firing at the high temperatures needed for porcelain making. The other type, which was strongly and magnificently developed in the second half of the century, sought to reproduce the spectacular polychromes not only of China but also of Japan: the Dutch had a monopoly of the Japanese trade, and were the sole importers of porcelain from Arita, which included both the Kakiemon and the Imari types, as well as large quantities of Japanese blue and white. All this was known as '*kraak porseleyn*' after ships in the Far Eastern trade called carracks.

In the blue and white wares, therefore, one finds at first the styles of the reign of Wan Li (1573–1619); and it has been held that the rise of the Delft industry was greatly helped by the shortage of porcelain due to the disturbance caused by the Manchu invasions following Wan Li's death. Designs were also taken from what have been called the 'Transition' wares, produced between that time and the accession of K'ang Hsi in 1662. Their landscapes and freely drawn plants and flowers, figures and birds, show a complete breakaway from the more formal work of the previous dynasty.

After this the Dutch painters ranged through most of the types of blue and white made by the K'ang Hsi potters. Perhaps the most famous producer of them was Aelbrecht Cornelisz. de Keyser. He was the first of the *plateelbakkers* to be elected to the Council of the St Luke's Guild, and the new-found dignity of the craft is seen in the fact that he has by now added a surname to the old-fashioned patronymic Corneliszoon. His work set a standard for the whole age.

Lambertus van Eenhorn of 'The Metal Pot', and Louwijs Fictoor of 'The Double Jug', the similarity of whose monograms has sometimes confused collectors, were excellent makers of blue and white, and some of the very finest has been credited to Ghisbrecht Lambrechtsz. Kruyck, of 'The Porcelain Dish' pottery. Some pieces in this blue and white class make use of the decorative scheme known as *trek*, whereby design is outlined in manganese purple and the detail added in blue perhaps in another hand. Some work of the type by Samuel van Eenhorn, of the 'Greek A' pottery, and bearing his initials, has fine colour and admirably free treatment of the figures. There was also black *trek*.

POLYCHROME IMITATIONS

As the potters turned over to imitation of the Chinese and Japanese polychromes they added new colours to their palette, including a yellow made from oxide of antimony, a green from a mixture of this and cobalt, and an iron-red which was virtually new to faience—the range of high-temperature colours was now orange, yellow, red, green, purple and black. These high-temperature colours were fired in the kiln along with the tin glaze, like the English delftwares. But there was an important difference between the processes. By the Dutch method, the piece was first fired or air-dried to 'leather hardness', and then covered in a tin glaze suspended in water. Being much more porous than the English body, the clay would soak up the water and leave the tin glaze as a powdery surface on which the high-temperature colours, mixed with a glassy flux, could be painted. The piece was then covered with *kwaart*, a fine dust of colourless lead glaze (like the Italian *coperta*). In the firing the colours were fused with the tin glaze and the lead glaze; thus giving that fine brilliant glaze and rich depth of colour which, at its best, made Dutch *porseleyn* almost indistinguishable from Chinese porcelain, and well justified the claim implied in the name.

Later, say from about 1720, the Delft men developed the art of enamelling, i.e., firing additional colours *over* the glaze in a low-temperature muffle kiln, thus making available the same pinks, lilacs, greys and opaque blues as were used by the porcelain makers of both the Far East and Europe.

Adriaen Pijnacker, a follower of his father-in-law, the Aelbrecht de Keyser already mentioned, favoured the Japanese rather than the Chinese styles, and in doing so became the outstanding master of *delft doré*, in which gilding is added to the polychromes, and also *delft noir*, where, as in the famous *famille noire* porcelain of China, the colours are thrown up from a ground of black—there are also fields of dark blue, olive, green and turquoise.

The subjects of these 'Dutch Oriental' wares were the usual dragons and gods, fantastic birds and rocks and trees. There were also the *lange lijsen* or 'long Elizas' seen in English delftware. There is indeed something akin to the English *chinoiserie* in the fancy with which the Dutch translated these Far Eastern decorative idioms into something peculiarly their own—less grand, perhaps, than the originals, but far more charming.

If Delft lay near the crossroads of trade from the Far East, and was strongly influenced by this fact, it was also the home of Jan Vermeer. By this time, oil painting and engraving was the supreme art of the Netherlands. The huge skies and the mellow light gave the artists an instinct for tonal landscapes, while the intimate life of the towns aroused a feeling for genre scenes. It would have been surprising if, now that the technical problems of fine painting on faience had been solved, this movement did not affect the pottery painters. After early attempts to combine a few Dutch subjects with the Chinese motifs, there began to arise a native style of faience painting both in blue monochrome and colour which was to become the Dutch *faienciers*' really original contribution to ceramics.

Some of their work is fit to stand comparison with that of the oil painters and engravers themselves. Best known of the delftware men—though identified only by two signed pieces—is Frederik van Frijtom, who was working at Delft

Dutch delft horse (Rijksmuseum, Amsterdam) *and bird tureen painted in polychrome, with marks of Jan Theunis Dextra.* $5\frac{1}{2}$ *in.*, c. *1760.* (Sotheby and Co.)

Panel painted in colours in baroque style with Chinese themes. (Victoria and Albert Museum.)

from 1658 to 1673, possibly for Lambertius Kleffius at 'The Metal Pot'. There are plates (p. 51) with wide plain rims and landscapes with a fine aerial perspective which seem to be in his style.

But the great majority of the work remains unidentified. There are scenes familiar to us from Dutch genre pictures—the skating groups, views in the towns, series showing ships in the herring fleet, goings-on in tavern and workshop, seascapes and harbour scenes. We see the interiors of houses, of schools and churches. There are also the famous music plates, some of which, like those made in Bristol, give us the only surviving text of songs once sung every day in home and tavern. Subjects from the Bible are frequently found, and there are also heraldic and floral designs in the contemporary baroque styles. These are to be seen not only on plates, but also on the large *garnitures de cheminée* imitated from the Chinese forms and usually consisting of three covered vases, and two trumpet-shaped beakers. The same decorations also appear on tobacco jars, cruet bottles and all manner of other wares.

Among the leaders in polychrome painting of Dutch subjects was Rochus Hoppesteyn, of 'The Young Moor's Head', using mainly blue with sparing use of other colours; while Gijsbrecht Verhaest, also employed by Hoppesteyn, painted panels in delicate colours. Much of this work expressed the European baroque themes as used at Meissen, Vienna and other porcelain centres in the early and mid eighteenth century.

Very distinctive was a form of decoration in five colours called *cachemire*, perhaps modelled on patterns of silks from Kashmir. Both Louwijs Fictoor and Lambertus van Eenhorn made use of this, but the latter is said to have been its originator. A complicated form of decoration which depends for its effect upon a skilful distribution of the forms and colours, it combines lambrequins with patterns in reserve, together with baskets of flowers, birds and figures.

'PEASANT' DELFT

One class of wares which has interested collectors increasingly in recent times is *boerendelftsch* or peasant delft. This is almost to be ranked with the everyday Staffordshire productions of the nineteenth century, aimed at the burgher and the farmer, using a broad style of decoration in monochrome blue or high-temperature colours. Simplified Chinese or European styles are used—sometimes inextricably mixed in a manner very much like that of similar wares made in northern France at this time. The two are often very difficult to distinguish. There is also 'sponged' decoration, as found on some English wares. As works of art or craftsmanship this class does not bear comparison with the great wares made for the luxury trade, but it has its own attractive qualities, a fact that was realized as long ago as 1872, when M. Marechal published some pictures of typical pieces in his *La Faience populaire*.

57 *Dutch delft pagoda, painted in blue, marked 'A.K.'. Height 3 ft 9 in. Late seventeenth or early eighteenth century.* (Victoria and Albert Museum.)

Among the paintings to be found in this class are portraits of members of the House of Orange which are strongly reminiscent of the royal portraits on our own 'blue-dash' chargers. There are also the usual Dutch ships, windmills, landscapes and river scenes. Many of these plates and dishes have their footrims pierced with holes, as do chargers, and they were evidently regarded as the peasant version of the more splendid plaque or tile picture. They were made not only in Delft, but in out-potteries at Makkum, Harlingen and Bolsward. Some of them are described as 'Lemmer-ware', after the Frisian port of Lemmer.

SHAPES AND FORMS

The potters of Delft were not great originators in matters of shape or form. Their *forte* lay in the fine quality of their earthenware and the decoration of its surface, and they seem to have been content to make their vases, beakers, jugs and other vessels in shapes copied directly either from the Far East or from the rococo and baroque forms pioneered in porcelain—for example, the tall pagodas (p. 57) and the triumphal arches with 'fingers' for flowers.

Many small novelties were made, as gifts or souvenirs, in the same spirit as is shown in Staffordshire wares of the era. There were pairs of shoes like those made in English delftware (p. 44) reflecting current fashions in the height of heels; also sledges for holding pipes and other items. Jugs in the form of monkeys, and hand-warmers disguised as books, usually prayer-books, were popular; so too was a small box which held burning peat, on which the tired housewife, kicking off her clogs, could rest and warm her stockinged feet. Most remarkable of all in this field perhaps were the complete birdcages, and the very rare violins.

As in many other wares, Dutch delft offered its quota of dishes modelled as birds, fruit and flowers: there were also the well-known cow milk jugs which are to be found in silver as well as Staffordshire earthenware. A Dutch speciality here seems to have been the 'pike' dish, in which that fish coils itself realistically on the cover in a remarkably *trompe l'œil* fashion.

Figures appear in Dutch delft, but here again the art of modelling seems to have been too much for most of the potters. There are parrots on rocks, adapted from K'ang Hsi porcelain: there are also some native versions perched upon rings. Cocks and hens are to be found, also frogs and horses, many of them crude imitations of Meissen. Figures (and also 'useful' wares) were made in the so-called *wit-delftsch*, the plain white delft of the seventeenth and eighteenth centuries, but the insipidity of most of the forms seems to call for the engaging irrelevance of the decoration found on the painted wares (p. 55).

Among the many kinds of 'useful' wares to be found in Dutch delft are fine soup and vegetable tureens, once the proud adornment of some burgher's table. There are shapely butter bowls, oil and vinegar stands, salt-cellars and pepper casters, on all of which the decoration is hardly less fine than on the wares made only for display. This also applies to the many kinds of tobacco and snuff jars, the cisterns made to hang on walls for washing one's hands in after a meal, even to spittoons and chamber pots.

TILES

Side by side with the growth of the fine Netherlands *porseleyn* made by the *plateelbakkers*, there was great activity in tile-making. It was virtually a separate industry, for the *tegelbakkers*, though not undertaking the work of the *plateel* men, sometimes made the heavy vessels called *schotel-goed*, which, like the tiles, did not call for the use of saggars to protect the wares in the kiln. From the latter part of the seventeenth century onwards Rotterdam, Haarlem, Amsterdam and Middleburg became the great centres of tile-making.

Tiles were always more popular for domestic purposes in the Netherlands than perhaps anywhere else, although these were used on walls rather than on floors, as was

usually the case in Italy and Spain. In kitchens, dairies and cellars they would perhaps cover the whole wall—there is a magnificent example of such a use of imported Dutch tiles in the Amalienburg pavilion at Nymphenburg, near Munich. In living-rooms they usually covered fireplaces or overmantels, pier walls or wainscotting, and they came in an astonishing variety, either singly or in combination, making up continuous patterns on walls.

Earliest of the Dutch tin-glazed tiles followed the styles of the Renaissance. Here one sees the rich grapes and the bursting pomegranates with parti-coloured leaves, as on Venetian maiolica. Some had single flowers—like the tulip which was to become a national obsession—or animals such as stags and hares: now also came the first of the flowers in vases. There was rich variety in the borders, with their corner fillings of *fleur de lys* or other forms, themselves creating a fine decorative discipline across a wall.

Dutch delft panel tile, 20 in. high. Delft, late seventeenth or early eighteenth century. (Victoria and Albert Museum.)

For colours the potters called upon the typical maiolica palette of blue, yellow, green and orange, with rare use of manganese purple. The patterns were usually outlined by 'pouncing', i.e. dusting charcoal through stencils pricked with holes. In the early tiles the body was reddish in colour and up to $\frac{5}{8}$ in. thick; later it was yellowish or light buff in colour and much thinner.

As with other wares the maiolica style was succeeded by native motifs and subjects. Towards the middle of the seventeenth century, the influence of Chinese imports brought a fashion for manganese purple and blue monochrome wares. But apart from the typical Wan Li key-fret used on borders, both Chinese motifs and *chinoiseries* are surprisingly rare. They are seen most often, perhaps, as part of the rococo mood.

For many collectors the most attractive work on these tiles of the later seventeenth century, fascinating in their variety and ingenuity, are the ships, the sea monsters and other mythical figures, the sketchily drawn landscapes with figures; also all the race of 'manikins'—the ladies and cavaliers, fishermen, farmers, priests and pedlars, musicians and tumblers, also the many charming groups of children. Biblical subjects abound, telling many of the old stories.

TILE PICTURES

These pictorial tiles were evidently intended to provide a kind of picture gallery for the humbler householder who could not afford the easel paintings collected by the wealthier classes. But the idea was carried a long way further in the complete tile picture, whereby whole compositions, sometimes very large, were made up from many separate pieces.

The earliest of them, as might be expected, are in the Netherlands maiolica styles, but in later days they followed the same motifs as in plates and dishes, adapting designs from engravings, even grouping them in frames, pilasters or columns and giving a striking architectural effect. In the

Victoria and Albert Museum there is a colossal panel made up of no fewer than 357 different tiles and painted in manganese purple with an allegorical subject after a design for a glass window in the Groote Kerk at Gouda.

Similarly, the usual flower and vase subjects would be built up into striking and handsome compositions, like the one shown here (p. 60), which is also in the Victoria and Albert. There are as well some rare attempts to imitate the *chinoiserie* wallpapers of the eighteenth-century rococo.

Less spectacular, but none the less engaging, are the smaller panels adapted from paintings or engravings of Dutch interiors and landscapes, which are given frames and set off in a surround of blank panels, as though they were actual pictures hanging on a wall. House signs of the potteries themselves were often made up in this way.

Towards the end of the eighteenth century the Dutch delft industry started to feel the keen wind of competition from new quarters, notably the creamware of Josiah Wedgwood and his English and Continental imitators. Throughout the second half of the century the Dutch had desperately tried to emulate the thin body and the fine highly detailed painting of the low-temperature colours in porcelain—for example, Meissen harbour scenes and Watteau subjects—and in doing so had lost a great deal of their own inimitable qualities and virtues. In the same

Delft tiles painted in blue and manganese purple, eighteenth century. (Victoria and Albert Museum.)

attempt to survive, the tile-making industry, facing the competition of the wallpapers now fashionable among the *bourgeoisie*, dropped its more explosive colours for monochrome blue or purple, and crowded its tiles with motifs which, though individually very fine, had lost the ability to combine on a wall.

By the early 1800s there were only ten of the original potteries left in Delft itself: the last one, 'The Three Bells', damped down its fires for the last time in 1850. Thirty years later another factory opened its doors in the town—but it was no longer to make wares painted on the dusty and absorbent tin glaze. Instead it used a hard-fired earthenware with painting done over a 'slip' or wet paste glaze. This product, nothing at all like the original, was, ironically enough, the first kind of pottery from the town of Delft to be called 'delftware'.

Apart from the above-mentioned manifestly different product, which would not deceive anybody having the slightest acquaintance with the real thing, there are other imitations which are rather harder to detect. A great deal of German blue and white faience of the seventeenth and eighteenth centuries, specifically the products of Frankfurt, which used the lead overglaze, has been mistaken for the work of Delft. The fact that manufacturers often omitted their own mark—a practice not at all uncommon among quite respectable English potters—did not help matters.

There are also deliberate reproductions of well-known styles, usually made in northern France, which have often deceived knowledgeable people by their very fair imitations of body, glaze and colour. Especially adept here, as in other fields, is the firm of Samson, of Paris, who have made excellent imitations of most European ceramic wares, but who usually—and now always, I believe—have added their own mark to their productions.

The seasoned collector will already have worked out his own safeguards in examining these imitations and forgeries. For the tyro, it needs only to say here, as in all fields of collecting, that there is no substitute for intimate familiarity with original work. In modern versions, or contemporary work done elsewhere, there is always some fatal flaw: the body is never quite of the same substance or consistency, the colours are never *really* accurate, the decoration invariably betrays the hand of a man or woman who is living in a different age or another environment. Marks can be of help sometimes, but being the easiest things of all to fake, they are to be relied on only after everything else has been proved 'right'.